THE
MEDIEVAL CHURCH
in Manuscripts

THE
MEDIEVAL CHURCH
in Manuscripts

JUSTIN CLEGG

THE BRITISH LIBRARY

Equiem eternam
dona eis domine.
et lux perpetua lu
ceat eis.

Comment len celebre loffice et le service de la messe pour les trespasses en priant dieu quil leur donne
vray repos et lumiere pardurable. Comte on se doit ordonner contre la mort. confesser. communier. et conseiller.

INTRODUCTION

During the Middle Ages, nothing dominated life in western Europe quite like the Church. In an age when the world was regarded as being divided into two broad spheres, namely the ecclesiastical, or Church, sphere and the secular, or worldly, sphere, many believed that the former was by far the more important. For the medieval world was a highly religious one, and the Church grew until it exercised a surprisingly diverse, and profound, influence upon the lives of the people of Europe (1). As an institution, the Late Medieval Church completely dwarfed its contemporaries. For a start, it was not constrained by

1. Prayerbook of King Alphonso V of Aragon, c. 1442, showing him attending mass with his family and courtiers. Even royalty surrendered centre stage to the Church, with the King reduced to the role of an onlooker in this scene in the royal chapel. Additional MS 28962, f. 281v.

existing political boundaries, since its power stretched from Scandinavia in the north to Sicily in the south, and from Iceland in the west to Poland in the east. Yet it was also one of the most organised institutions in Europe, for below the pope, who sat at its head, was a well-staffed Church government, complete with chancery, treasury and law court. Under this was an extremely large and elaborate hierarchy of appointed staff, from cardinal through to priest, that enabled the Church to reach from the papal palace into the smallest village. Medieval society recognised the importance of the Church as an institution by making a basic but fundamental

2. The preservation of knowledge: Saint Jerome writing, depicted as an Augustinian monk. So-called Worms Bible, dated 1148, from Frankenthal, Germany. Harley MS 2803, f. 1v.

distinction between the clergy, who were members of it, and the laity, who were not.

The Church also had a profound effect upon secular society, and played an important part in a range of areas. For instance, the Church performed a wide variety of social roles, such as running hospitals for the sick, providing hostels for travellers and distributing relief to the poor. In the area of education the medieval Church was especially important. During the so-called Dark Ages the Church was the only beacon of knowledge in Western Europe, preserving Christendom's written heritage within its churches and monasteries – which helps to explain why images of the clerical writer at work, such as the picture of Saint Jerome at the beginning of the Worms Bible (2), are common. In fact, the Church held a virtual monopoly on education until the emergence of the universities in the late twelfth century, and continued to play an important role throughout the period. The Church was the driving force behind medieval Europe's intellectual development, extending the boundaries of knowledge in everything from arithmetic to zoology. Moreover, churchmen provided the kings and princes of Europe with their best government officials, for the Church produced skilled and educated administrators in an age when such people were in short supply.

However, these aspects should not distract us from the Church's primary functions, which were to minister to the religious and spiritual needs of the Christianised people of Europe, and to spread the Word of God to the unconverted (3).

3. *Archbishop Peter of Aix, preaching, in an early fifteenth-century English copy of his biblical commentary, entitled* Compendium Super Bibliam. *Royal MS 8 G iii, f. 2.*

Below: 4. *Ecclesia personified, holding a church, from an English psalter, c. 1310–1320. Additional MS 49622, f. 128v.*

Before the Protestant Reformation of the sixteenth century, the religious authority of the institution now known as the Catholic, or Roman, Church was essentially unchallenged in the West. People at the time simply referred to it as 'The Church', or *ecclesia* if they knew any Latin, since there was no other (4). For people were taught that the pope was Christ's representative on Earth and that his Church was the only legitimate successor to the Church of the Apostles. As a result, the faithful believed that they could only find salvation for their souls, and thus avoid damnation in the afterlife, by following the teachings of the Church. The Church was therefore regarded as the gateway to redemption for everyone, from sovereign to serf. From birth until death, it was the Church that provided the framework within which people lived their lives, and its festivals shaped their year.

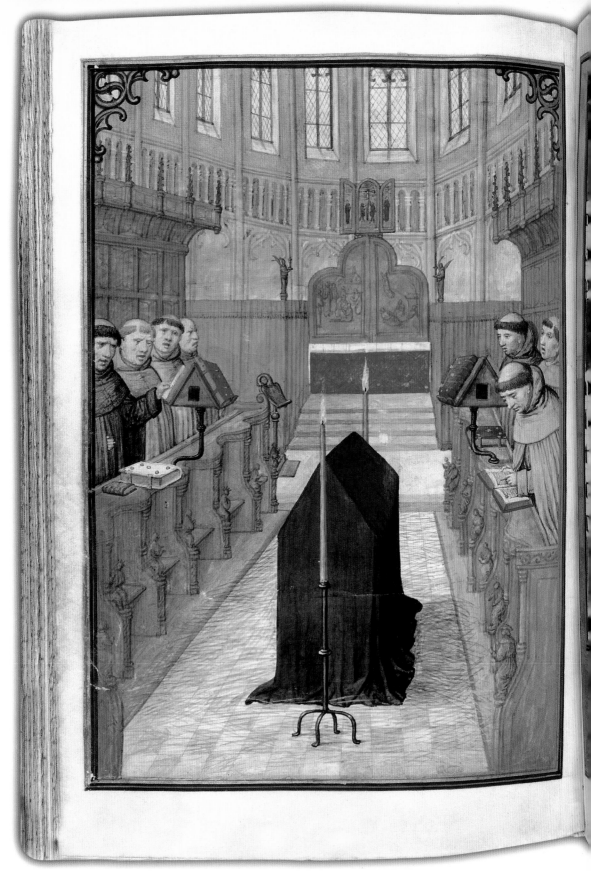

We can gain a glimpse of the medieval Church in the cathedrals, monasteries and churches that continue to dominate many of Europe's cities, towns and villages. Its material remains can also be seen in museums and art galleries, which display some of the metalwork, sculpture, artwork and textiles that were such a feature of daily religious life. But most of the buildings have been stripped of their medieval decorations and ornaments, whilst the items held in museums are like pieces in a jigsaw puzzle and provide a fragmentary picture of the past. Yet the world of the medieval Church is vividly brought to life in illuminated manuscripts. Because so many medieval illuminated books were made for the purpose of religious devotion, they frequently contain images relating to the Church of the Middle Ages. Moreover, the images survive in great number, and are often in excellent condition, since a single book can sometimes contain hundreds of images, protected from damage within closed covers. But their most important contribution is that they often provide a more complete picture of this vanished world than other sources. The funeral scene in a prayerbook that was probably made for Joanna of Ghistelles, who became abbess of Messines in 1516, is a fine example, for it provides information relating to ceremony, dress, ornament and architecture in a single image (5).

Obviously, a book of this size cannot expect to provide a comprehensive treatment of the Church in Western Europe during the Middle Ages, since there were considerable developments during the 1,000 or so years of its medieval existence, and significant regional differences in custom and practice. As a result, this work concentrates upon the later Middle Ages, which saw the medieval Church reach its most developed, glorious and, arguably, most flawed form with its emphasis on elaborate ceremonial and show. It has also often proved necessary to resort to broad generalities, many of which only apply to the Church in England. But, although a broad brush has been used, and the canvas is small, the resulting picture should capture something of the medieval Church's spirit.

Opposite page: 5. Funeral service being conducted before the high altar of a church, with monks singing in their choir stalls. Flemish prayerbook of Joanna of Ghistelles, c. 1516. Egerton MS 2125, f. 117v.

CHURCH STRUCTURE
POPE, CARDINALS AND CURIA

The medieval Church was a highly centralised and hierarchical structure. At its head was a single figure, the pope, the 'Supreme Pontiff', or bridge builder between man and God, and 'Christ's Vicar', or representative, on Earth, whose succession could be traced back to Peter the Apostle. Because Jesus described Saint Peter as custodian of the keys to the kingdom of heaven, and the rock upon which the Church would be built, his successors, who adopted the title Bishop of Rome, successfully championed their right to lead the Western Church. The Bishop of Rome therefore acquired the role of Father of the Church, or *papa* in Latin, hence pope. As a result, the pope became the ultimate authority on matters of faith and morals, and was commonly regarded as a figure whose appointment and subsequent pronouncements were divinely inspired. Moreover, it was the pope who controlled the appointment of senior ecclesiastical figures and acted as judge in serious ecclesiastical disputes. Even though lesser appointments and minor judgements were usually made at a lower level, the pope argued that this was a delegation of responsibility and jealously guarded the right

6. *Pope pronouncing excommunication, with a bell, book and candle, from an English encyclopaedia, c. 1360–1375. Royal MS 6 E vi, f. 216v.*

to ratify or rescind the decisions of those it had appointed (6). But he was not free to act as he wished, for his decisions had to be acceptable to the wider community of the Church. When the Church was faced with serious challenges to its teachings or authority, or when it was thought necessary to make major changes to Church doctrine or practice, the pope would summon a general Church council, composed of senior ecclesiastical figures, as well as theologians and experts in Church, or canon, law.

7. *The pope, attended by cardinals, receiving a delegation, in a Bohemian copy of the* Travels of Sir John Mandeville, *c. 1410. Additional MS 24189, f. 7v.*

However, major Church councils were extremely uncommon, with only seventeen of those held before the year 1500 being regarded as ecumenical, or universal and completely binding. Instead, when the pope had to make less sweeping but important changes he increasingly relied upon the opinion of the cardinals. The office of cardinal originally appeared in order to help the pope with his duties as Bishop of Rome. But as the Church grew in size, and the role of the pope grew in importance, so too did the power of the cardinals until, by the end of the medieval period, they outranked all but the pope. The cardinals, whose number was set at a maximum of seventy, advised the pope on matters of faith and discipline during regular consistories, or meetings, and acted as his representatives beyond the walls of the papal palace (7). After the third Lateran Council of 1179 they were exclusively charged with the responsibility of electing the pope, and in 1409 were forced to call a council to depose two rival popes so as to resolve a longstanding division of authority, or schism. As a result, the cardinals were in a position to challenge papal excess. Yet true authority always resided in the figure of the pope, for it was the pope who appointed bishops to be cardinals, and the cardinals owed allegiance to the pope as head of the Church.

8. The Curia, with pope, cardinals and administrative officials, depicted in a fourteenth-century Italian copy of Pope Gregory IX's popular work on ecclesiastical law, known as the Decretals. Additional MS 23923, f. 2

As the medieval Church expanded, until it covered thousands of square miles and tens of millions of people, it became apparent that the pope and cardinals needed administrative support. As a result, a papal government, known as the Curia, soon evolved (8). The curia changed and grew throughout the Middle Ages, but it eventually consisted of a complex collection of departments based in and around the papal palace. Each section, which was either staffed or managed by cardinals, was charged with a particular area of responsibility, and dealt with cases from all over Europe, with only the most important business being passed to the consistory or pope. But the truly impressive aspect was the breadth of the curia's responsibilities, which included administrative, disciplinary, financial, judicial and theological matters.

By the Late Middle Ages, the institution of the papacy, composed of pope, cardinals and curia, had become the most important administrative force within the Church, for it controlled the Church down to the level of the parish and exercised its control throughout Europe. The papacy also became one of the richest institutions, because the church was Europe's largest landowner, and the pope claimed his share of the revenue. When a new appointment was made or confirmed, the papacy claimed the first year's income relating to the post, known as an annate. In addition, it appropriated revenue from vacant posts until someone had been chosen to fill them. The papacy also received payments from other sources, including England's contribution of Peter's Pence, which regularly provided the papacy with the sum of £200 per annum, until abolished by Henry VIII in 1534. As a result, the papacy provided the Church with a powerful, and wealthy, administrative head, below which the institutional body of the Church split into two parts, known as the Secular Church and the Regular Church (9).

9. This image from a record book made at New Minster, Winchester, c. 1031 identifies the two groupings of the Regular and Secular Church by showing an abbot and a bishop. Stowe MS 944, f. 6v.

CHURCH STRUCTURE
THE SECULAR CHURCH

The larger and more important of the two groups that formed the medieval Church is occasionally referred to as the Secular Church, from the Latin word *saecula*, meaning world. The term Secular Church is useful because it allows us to differentiate between the Regular clergy, who took vows that separated them from society and originally lived in secluded monasteries, and the Secular clergy, who served the structured day-to-day religious needs of the people. However, although useful, the term is ultimately misleading, for it gives the impression that the Secular Church and Regular Church were somehow equally important. This was far from the case, for the Secular clergy were essential for the performance of the Church's duties, unlike the Regular clergy. The Secular clergy provided the bones of Christ's Church on Earth, and its complex hierarchy of archbishops, bishops and priests formed the body of the Church and allowed it to function. The Regular Church, however, was a limb of the Church, since it received its authority from the Secular clergy (10). The hierarchy of Secular clergy provided the essential administrative structure of the Church, allowing Christendom to be divided into increasingly smaller and more manageable geographical units.

10. *This bishop blessing an abbess, in a French pontifical of the early fourteenth century, indicates the Secular clergy's authority over the Regular clergy. Additional MS 39677, f. 47.*

At the top of this administrative structure were the archbishops, or metropolitans, who exercised control over districts known as provinces. England was divided into the provinces of Canterbury and York, with the two archbishops taking precedence over bishops in the south and north of England respectively. Below the archbishop were the bishops, who supervised the dioceses, but although the archbishop had jurisdiction over the bishops of his province, he was essentially a bishop, and also managed his own diocese, known as an archdiocese. Indeed, the church buildings in which both the archbishops and bishops had their administrative seats were called cathedrals, from *cathedra*, meaning chair, since they exercised the same religious authority (11). Both the archdioceses and dioceses were further split into administrative units known as archdeaconries and rural deaneries, headed by

11. This wonderfully detailed image of an Archbishop of the mid-thirteenth century in full vestments, shows him as he would have appeared whilst performing his official religious duties. Illustration, c.1250, added on a blank leaf in an English psalter, originally made c.1200. Royal MS 2 A xxii, f.221.

archdeacons and deans, who were answerable to the archbishop or bishop. Below this was the fundamental administrative unit, known as the parish, which was headed by a priest. This ecclesiastical structure was established throughout Europe, allowing the Church to break Christendom into administrative blocks according to geographical size and density of population. For instance the English bishopric of Ely was fairly small, both in terms of territory and population, since it was sandwiched between the bishoprics of London, Lincoln and Norwich. As a result, it had only one archdeacon. On the other hand, the bishopric of Lincoln extended from the river Humber to Oxford, and was divided into eight archdeaconries.

The division of the Church into administrative units was an important achievement. For one thing it provided an effective means of communication between pope and priests, whether in Dublin or Dubrovnic. It also allowed the Church to monitor and regulate itself, for the pope could check up on the archbishops by sending cardinals to visit the provinces. The bishops usually relied on their archdeacons, but could also undertake personal tours, or visitations. This allowed the Church to determine whether its representatives were able to perform their diocesan and parochial, or parish, duties. Thus the bishop ensured that the clergy of the diocese performed their duties, and that those who failed were either fined in his court or dismissed from office. Moreover, it enabled the Church to delegate certain responsibilities and duties. For instance, bishops were not only empowered to deal with minor infringements of canon law in their own ecclesiastical courts, but were also authorised to ordain priests. Indeed, the religious

12. Ordination: German pontifical of the late fifteenth century showing a subdeacon receiving the tunicle garment from a bishop. Additional MS 14805, f. 17v.

13. Marginal scenes showing infant baptism and absolution following confession, from a French Book of Hours, late fifteenth century. Confession and absolution formed part of the sacrament of Penance. Egerton MS 2019, f. 135.

duties of a bishop were often gathered into a single book, known as a pontifical, many of which were lavishly decorated (12). The true importance of this hierarchy was that it allowed the Secular Church to perform its ecclesiastical religious duties. The parish clergy typically served the religious needs of the people by saying mass, performing marriages and baptisms, hearing confessions and providing absolution (13), administering the last rites and conducting funerals. But the bishop controlled some rites and procedures, such as Confirmation and the consecration of church buildings (14, overleaf). As a result, the hierarchy was essential for the conduct of the Church's religious responsibilities.

At the close of the medieval period, the terms and titles within the Secular Church had become bewildering, with clerics employed in a variety of roles, including chantry priest, canon, chaplain and confessor. Yet the Church essentially recognised only two broad divisions within the Secular clergy, known as Minor Orders and Major Orders. The Minor Orders included the ranks of porter, lector, exorcist and acolyte, whilst the Major Orders contained those of subdeacon, deacon, priest and bishop. Each order was a clerical rank that had to be undertaken in sequence, beginning with that of porter, and the process began with the act of tonsure, during which the top of the cleric's head was shaved as a visible sign of his religious calling. In the eyes of the Church, the main difference between the two was that those in Minor Orders, or minorities, did not commit themselves to a life of celibacy, and could therefore leave the

14. *A bishop consecrating a church, from the Benedictional of St Æthelwold, c. 970–980. This book contained the benedictions, or blessings, that a bishop would say during certain services, and was made for Æthelwold, bishop of Winchester. Additional MS 49598, f. 118v.*

Church and marry at any time without penalty. Those in Major Orders, on the other hand, were expected to have made a lifelong commitment to the Church and therefore needed permission, known as a dispensation, in order to leave. However, the real difference between the various ranks of the clergy rested on the duties that they were able to perform. The sacrament of Confirmation was usually conducted by a bishop, whilst the sacrament of the Eucharist, performed during the Mass, was reserved for those who had at least been ordained priests (15).

By the fifteenth century the number of people entering Minor Orders had become considerable. Many people simply saw Minor Orders as the first step towards a professional career, even if they intended to find secular employment as government administrators or lawyers. The practice became so common that the medieval English term 'clerk', meaning someone who had at least taken Minor Orders, soon came to be applied to anyone who had received a basic formal education, and survives to this

15. *A bishop conducting the sacrament of Confirmation within his cathedral, from a French pontifical of the late fifteenth century. Egerton MS 1067, f. 12.*

day as a general term for an administrator. In fact only a small number of people continued on to Major Orders. Some people were undoubtedly put off by the need to commit to a celibate life, even though they may have been interested in pursuing a religious vocation. But the main reason was that the opportunity for professional employment within the Church was limited, since salaried posts, called 'benefices', or 'livings', were not numerous. In England and Wales there were around 8,800 parishes in the late fifteenth century, each of which could probably support two or three clerics (16), so it has been suggested that the total number of people who were able to earn their living as Secular clerics in the English Church was about 25,000. As a result, most people who were interested in a clerical career waited until they secured a benefice before proceeding to Major Orders. The younger sons of the aristocracy could sometimes rely on securing extremely lucrative benefices, and were occasionally appointed before they had reached the accepted canonical age for the post. All of this helped to undermine the status of Minor Orders. On the one hand, many who undertook them had no real intention of going on to Major Orders, whilst, on the other, those who wished to pass beyond Minor Orders viewed them as an inconvenient formality and progressed through them quickly, often in a matter of days.

16. *Priest saying mass, with a Minor cleric in attendance. Book of Hours, England, mid-fifteenth century. Harley MS 2915, f. 84.*

The Secular Church of the Late Middle Ages was indeed a professional as well as a religious institution, for it was expected that its members would be supported either by the communities that they served, or by money accruing to the Church that was redistributed. In addition, members of the clergy were subject to ecclesiastical rather than secular authority and could therefore appeal to be judged in a Church court. Because ecclesiastical courts typically handed down sentences that were more lenient than those imposed by secular judges, this right understandably became known as 'benefit of clergy'. A common punishment for moderately serious crimes would have been 'degradation', which resulted in the guilty party being expelled from the clergy. However, the benefit was much abused during the later Middle Ages. For the ability to quote certain Latin psalms, such as 'Conserva me Domine', which formed part of the tonsure ceremony, or 'Miserere mei', which was an appeal to divine forgiveness, was often accepted as proof of clerical status by the secular courts. As a result, such passages were occasionally referred to as 'neck verse', for they could quite literally save the necks of those who had learned to recite them. But, although authorised to deal with serious crimes, the bishop's court mainly dealt with minor cases, such as inappropriate clerical behaviour. Images of clerical misbehaviour often appear as scenes in the margins of illuminated manuscripts, such as the Flemish item shown here (17), but their frequent employment probably stemmed from their comic value as amusing scenes, rather than an indictment of widespread clerical misconduct.

17. A marginal scene from a Maastricht Book of Hours, c. 1300, showing clerical misbehaviour, with a nun dancing to a tune played by a friar. Stowe MS 17, f. 38.

CHURCH STRUCTURE
THE REGULAR CHURCH

The second of the Church's main branches was often referred to as the Regular Church, since its members followed an authorised 'rule', which regulated the way in which they conducted their lives. Although the Regular Church followed a variety of individual rules, certain features soon became common to all. Thus, by the end of the twelfth century, the Regular clergy lived in communities, and took vows of chastity, poverty and obedience. As a result, they could not marry, could not own more than basic personal possessions and had to surrender their wills to the rigors of the rule. This contrasted with the Secular clergy, for although Secular clerics in Major Orders also adopted a life of celibacy, they could own private property, were not obliged to live in communities and only owed obedience to their superiors. In addition, the Regular clergy followed a far more austere life than their Secular Church cousins, for the rule typically laid down a strict regime of prayer, study and manual labour. They even went so far as to detail the day-to-day and hourly duties of the Regular clergy. Thus the Rule of Saint Benedict, which was one of the earliest and most influential of the rules, set the time of communal prayer, provided dietary regulations and otherwise described how the community's members should conduct themselves. It also describes how the monastery should be staffed, with officers such as the abbot, at its head, and the cellarer, in charge of provisions (18).

Although most members of the Regular Church had acquired clerical status by the second half of the Middle Ages, they were heirs to a movement that

18. Adam, cellarer of St Albans c. 1380, with the keys to the stores, as seen in one of the Abbey's record books, containing images of the community's members and benefactors. Cotton MS Nero D vii, f. 16v.

was originally independent of the Church. For in Christianity's first centuries, certain people decided to withdraw from society and devote themselves to prayer, either individually or collectively. The movement, which came to be known as monasticism, included individuals and communities, but the communal form eventually became the dominant form in Western Europe, until the term monk became synonymous with those who lived the 'common life'. By the Early Middle Ages monasticism had become fairly widespread, with communities scattered across Europe. More importantly, it had captured the popular imagination, since many regarded monastic communities as particularly religious institutions. People began to make donations of land and money in the hope that the monks would intercede with God on their behalf when they said their prayers. Some parents even dedicated children as young as ten to the monastery, handing them over to the monks together with endowments of land and money for the child's upkeep (19).

19. Parents handing a young child into the care of a monastery, from a copy of the Decretals of Pope Gregory IX, Italy, mid-fourteenth century. Additional MS 24642, f. 80v.

As a result of this growing popularity, the Church authorities began to take a greater interest in the movement. At first, this took the form of guidance and assistance, with individual bishops playing a role in the foundation and regulation of monasteries within their diocese. But as the power of the papacy grew, so too did papal interference in monastic affairs, until the monastic movement was eventually absorbed into the Church. As a result, the members of the Regular orders acquired clerical status. In return, the heads of the religious communities surrendered to papal authority. Yet they continued to run their own affairs and appoint their own leaders. Moreover, their clerical status was restricted, since it did not mean that they could automatically perform the functions of the Secular clergy. Consequently, the Regular and Secular clergy remained distinct groups (20).

Because monasticism was often inspired by individuals, or by the success of monasteries in particular locations, it was a rather complex and disjointed movement, composed of separate groupings known as Monastic Orders. The bewildering variety of medieval monastic orders bears testimony to this process. There were the monastic orders of the Benedictines and Augustinians, which were named after individuals who inspired their foundation, as well as those of the Carthusians, Cluniacs and Premonstatensians, which were originally founded at Chartreuse, Cluny and Prémontré. Moreover, each monastic order had its own administrative structures, terminologies and nicknames. The confusing legacy of this can still be detected in English place names, especially within London, such as Blackfriars (Dominican house), Greyfriars (Franciscan house), Abbey (main house), Priory (lesser, or dependant, house), Charterhouse (Carthusian main house) and even Temple (Templar house). Some of these names, such as Blackfriars and Greyfriars, bear testament to an area that can still cause confusion, namely the variety of dress, or habit, adopted by the individual orders. The Bible of William of Devon (21, overleaf) depicts four pairs of figures, of which the top two are easily identified as Franciscans and Dominicans, in grey and black. A third pair, in striped garments of brown and cream, are slightly harder to identify, until one remembers that the Carmelites wore striped garments before adopting a predominantly white dress in 1287, after which they were popularly known as the White Friars. The fourth pair is more problematic, for they have been identified as Friars of Blessed Mary de Arens, or Pied Friars, but are probably members of an order known as the Trinitarians.

20. Six roundels, surrounding scenes from Christ's life, showing saints in the dress of Secular bishops (top), Regular friars (middle) and Regular abbesses (bottom). Cutting from a Flemish psalter, late thirteenth century. Additional 28784 B, f. 5.

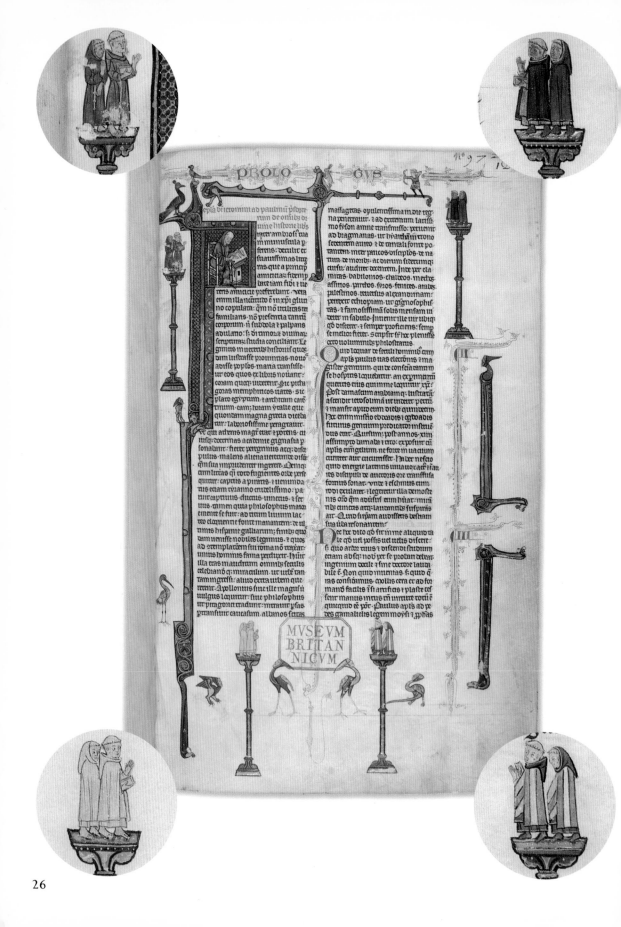

Despite the variety of names, the Regular clergy can be divided into three main groups, often referred to as the monastic, mendicant and military orders. The monastic orders were the largest of the three, and were characterised by their common desire to separate themselves from the secular world as far as was possible, retiring to the cloister and living in monasteries that were built away from existing towns and cities. They could not own personal possessions, but could share ownership of property, including land and money, within the community.

22. *A marginal scene from the Luttrell Psalter, England, c. 1325–1335, of a Franciscan friar hearing a nun's confession. Additional MS 42130, f. 74.*

The mendicant orders, from the Latin word *mendicare*, to beg, arose in the thirteenth century as a reaction to what were seen as weaknesses in the existing monastic movement. Its members, known as friars, could not own possessions either personally or even in common, but instead had to rely upon begging and charitable donations. Moreover, although they were separated from society by their vows, they worked amongst the people, preaching and hearing confession (22). As a result, the four mendicant orders of Dominicans, Franciscans, Carmelites and Augustinians usually built their friaries in urban areas. The military orders, the most famous of which were known as the Templars and Hospitallers, owed their origins and popularity to the crusading movements of the twelfth and thirteenth centuries.

Opposite page: 21. An English bible, c. 1260–1270, showing Franciscans (top left), Dominicans (top right), possibly Trinitarians (bottom left) and Carmelites (bottom right). Royal MS 1 D i, f. 1.

They qualified as Regular orders because their members followed a rule, but their membership was always small. Yet they testify to the flexible way in which the Regular life could be employed during the Middle Ages.

But one aspect of the Regular Church does cause considerable confusion. This is the degree to which the Regular Church became incorporated into the Secular Church. In the Early Middle Ages it was not unusual for monks to be ordained as priests and bishops, since the demand for Secular clerics frequently exceeded supply. An example of this is Saint Guthlac, a venerated Benedictine monk whose elevation to the priesthood is recorded in an illustrated roll commemorating his life (23). The process could be taken a stage further, for some monastic foundations were given dual status as Secular and Regular institutions. This was the case, for example, with the monasteries of Durham, Bath and Norwich, which became cathedral priories following reforms introduced by the Normans. The cathedral priory was a monastic foundation whose titular head, or abbot, was an archbishop, for the monastery provided a base from which to administer a diocese and therefore housed the bishop's throne or *cathedra*. However, the archbishop's monastic deputy, the prior, had practical control of the foundation, hence the term cathedral priory, rather than abbey. The process was taken to its logical conclusion by the order of Augustinian Canons Regular – a monastic order not related to the order of Augustinian Friars – as all its members were ordained clerics, and many were priests, which meant that they were both Secular and Regular clerics.

Although the boundary between the two was extremely blurred, the Regular Church ultimately provided an institutional alternative to the Secular Church. Indeed, for the religiously inclined woman of the Middle Ages the Regular Church provided the only opportunity to acquire clerical status. Since the Secular Church did not allow women to take the tonsure, let alone join the priesthood, the only alternative open to them was the veil. In other words, they could adopt the dress, or habit and veil, of a nun by joining a female community. Some of these communities were founded by women for women and led to the establishment of Regular orders that were exclusively female, as was the case with the Bridgettine Order, founded by Saint Bridget of Sweden. Others were founded by men as female offshoots of male orders, such as the Poor Clares (24, overleaf), who formed the Second Order of St Francis. A few had far more complex origins and structures. The Gilbertine Order, founded

23. Guthlac being ordained a priest by Bishop Hedda, from a roll depicting scenes from the life of St Guthlac, England, c. 1210. Harley Roll Y 6, roundel 11.

24. Miniature, c. 1420, showing Poor Clares seated in a choir stall, added to complete the decoration of a French psalter, made c. 1400–1410. Cotton MS Domitian A xvii, f. 74v.

by a priest called Gilbert at Sempringham in Lincolnshire, started out as a strictly female community. But their houses soon included a male component made up of Augustinian Canons and servants, called lay brothers. The former acted as chaplains to the nuns whilst the latter undertook the hard manual work. Yet, despite this variety, the female orders still shared certain features, since they were composed of one or more communities, commonly called convents or nunneries, which were governed by a rule.

Unfortunately, the female orders never attained the size or prestige of their male counterparts. Once again, the Gilbertine structure is of particular interest, for it opted to include male canons and lay brothers because the female religious were not authorised to perform the sacraments and found it hard to farm the land without assistance. In fact all nunneries had to employ, or otherwise support, priests if they

Opposite page: 25. Priests accompanying nuns in their religious observances. The nuns are only able to perform marginal duties, ringing the nunnery bells and carrying candles in the procession. French copy, c.1300 of a treatise on monasticism entitled La Sainte Abbaye. Yates Thompson MS 11, f. 6v.

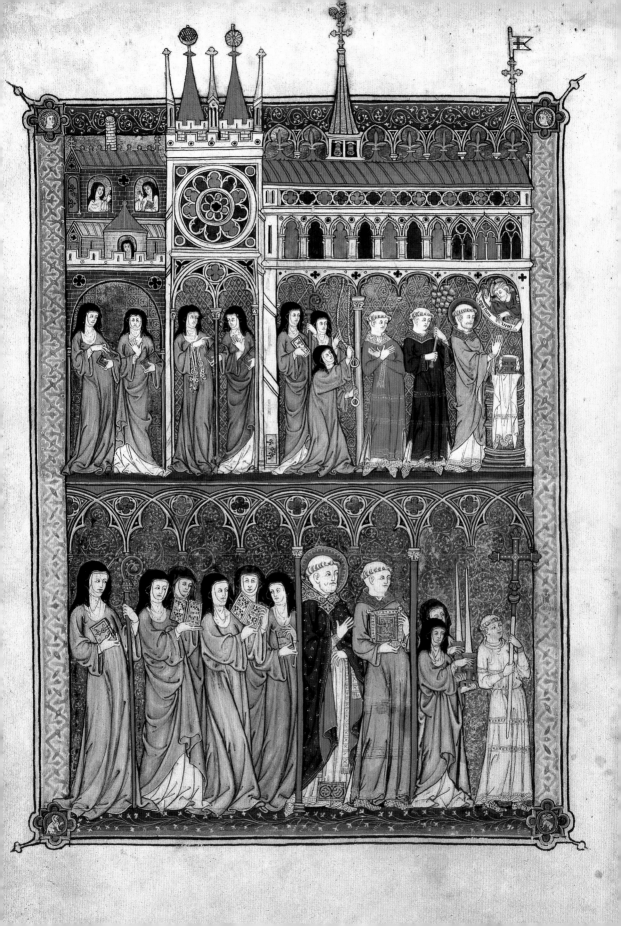

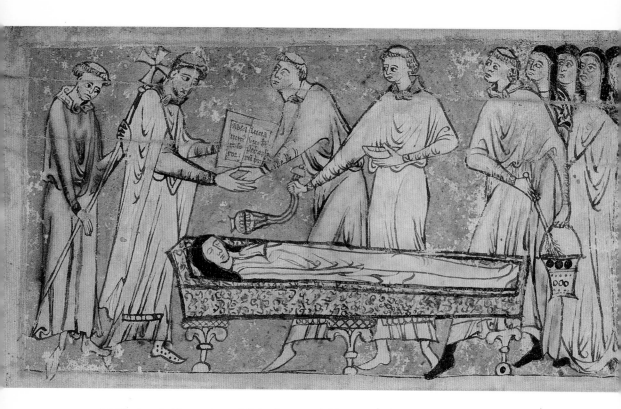

26. *The funeral of Lucy, prioress of Hedingham, attended by a priest, clerics and nuns. Roll commemorating Lucy de Vere, England, c. 1226. Egerton MS 2849.*

wished to celebrate the sacraments – as captured in an image from a treatise known as the *Sainte Abbaye*, showing male clerics leading nuns in prayer (25). They were also often forced to hire labour or lease their land because they could not farm it themselves. Worse still, nunneries rarely received the same level of donations as their male counterparts. All of this meant that convents were usually far poorer than male houses. Even so, many nuns and nunneries were well regarded. Lucy de Vere, founder and first prioress of the Benedictine nunnery of Hedingham, Essex, was so esteemed that a document commemorating her life, known as a mortuary, or death, roll contains entries from 122 religious houses in southern England (26).

CHURCH AND LAITY
SACRAMENT, CEREMONY AND SHOW

Although important, the structure of the Church only existed so as to allow it to perform its religious duties. At a fairly early date these duties were divided into separate elements that became established as the seven sacraments of Baptism, Confirmation, Eucharist, Penance, Orders, Matrimony and Extreme Unction. Each one of these sacraments represented a stage in the relationship between the faithful and God, from birth (baptism) to death (extreme unction, or last rites), and were administered by those suitably ordained within the Church. But it was not necessary to undergo all of the sacraments. Orders was restricted to those who had decided to become members of the clergy, since it related to clerical ordination (27), whilst Matrimony and Orders were, on the whole, mutually exclusive, since practising priests were not allowed to marry. But the other sacraments played a part in the lives of all Christians, whether cleric or layman, male or female. Most were typically undertaken once, the exceptions being Penance and the Eucharist, since it was expected that the faithful would seek absolution for their

27. A scene from a French pontifical, or bishop's service book, c. 1380, showing a bishop conducting the sacrament of the Eucharist for newly ordained priests.
Yates Thompson MS 24, f. 76.

33

sins and attend mass on a regular basis. According to the Church, the sacraments were religious and spiritual acts, undertaken by, or on behalf of, the individual. Yet the power of the Church was such that by the Late Middle Ages some had become obligatory social acts. This was the case with Baptism, for if a parent had failed to have his child baptised it would have had severe social, as well as religious, consequences. Similarly, matrimony assumed a social dimension, for although weddings contracted without a priest were quite legal, it became increasingly common, especially amongst the aristocracy, for those getting married to ask a priest to conduct the ceremony as a sacrament (28).

28. This scene from a Flemish copy of an historical work called the Chronique d'Angleterre, c. 1470–1483, shows the Church wedding of Waleran, Comte de St Pol, and bears witness to the growing popularity of matrimony. Royal MS 14 E iv, f. 39.

By the end of the medieval period most of the sacraments had become acts of high ceremonial and display. The rituals were elaborate, and the clergy wore ornate vestments, which were often brightly coloured and covered in embroidery (29). In addition, the ceremonies often involved the use of highly decorated utensils and items of furniture. These included the chalice and paten, a cup and plate for holding the wine and bread, or host, during the mass. These vessels were so important that they needed to be blessed, usually by a bishop, before they could be used.

Other ceremonial utensils included the ciborium, for storing the communion, the pyx, typically used for transferring the host to those unable to attend mass, and the monstrance, or ostensorium, for displaying the host in the church or during processions. Of course illustrated manuscripts also played a part, for many were produced so as to be of use during Church ceremonies. A processional from Norwich includes a diagram that shows the position of the priests during the service for Palm Sunday as though viewed from above. The circles represent the shaved heads

29. *An English lectionary, c. 1408, showing a Corpus Christi procession, with the bishop carrying the monstrance below a portable canopy, or baldachin. Such richly embroidered fabrics were extremely uncommon and would have created a powerful effect upon those viewing the ceremony. Harley MS 7026, f. 13.*

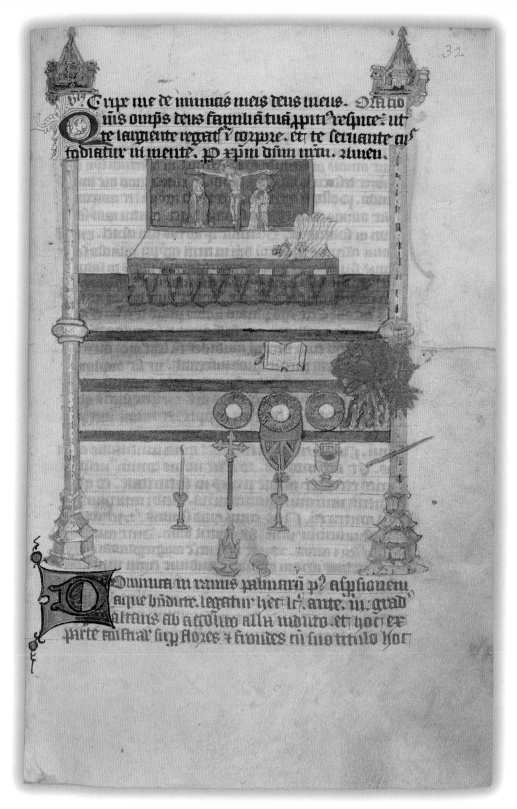

30. Diagram representing part of the service for Palm Sunday, from an English processional, c. 1400. *Additional MS 57534, f. 32.*

of the clerics, whilst the coloured triangle indicates the vestments worn by the officiating priest. The candlesticks and other items represent the position of the Minor clerics (30).

However, the most visible products of the medieval Church's liking for show and display were its buildings. The grandest were the cathedrals, for in an age when nearly all buildings were constructed of wood, and rarely had more than two storeys, they dominated the skylines of Europe's cities. To this day, their size and beauty are breathtaking, but in the Middle Ages they must have been, as their builders intended, nothing short of awesome. Of course time and changing tastes have not been kind to many of them, so it is necessary to remember that they were often highly coloured buildings, not only inside but out, with richly coloured stained glass and painted statues. But even so, they still impress today. Even the parish churches are striking, especially since they served the needs of small villages. This is one area where illustrations are less valuable for those interested in the medieval Church, for although they can provide information relating to their construction and ornamentation, the buildings need to be seen to be appreciated (31).

31. *King Offa overseeing the construction of St Albans' Abbey, from the* Lives of the Offas, *England, mid-thirteenth century. Cotton MS Nero D i, f. 23v.*

CHURCH AND LAITY
THE CALENDAR OF THE CHURCH

To a great extent, the modern calendar still betrays the Church's influence upon medieval society. For a start, the initial date from which we count our years was a medieval idea. But to fully appreciate the Church's influence we need to look at the medieval calendar, for although it may seem familiar it was, in fact, quite different. The most important date in the medieval calendar, as indeed it still is for the Church, was the festival of Easter. This formed the annual commemoration of Christ's death and resurrection, which was preceded by a forty-day period of fasting called Lent. Due to a variety of reasons the date of Easter needs to be established by complex calculations based on the lunar calendar (32). As a result, it does not have a fixed date, but can fall on any day from 22nd March to the 25th April. A whole host of important festivals, including Palm Sunday,

32. Clerics studying the computus, used for establishing the date of Easter, in an early fourteenth-century copy of a treatise on Church practice by William Durandus, entitled Rationale Divinorum Officiorum. Additional MS 31032, f. 1.

Pentecost, Ascension and Corpus Christi, depend upon the date of Easter and were subject to being moved within the solar calendar, giving rise to the expression 'moveable feast' (33). To those brought up with the modern concept of Christmas, the importance of Easter and its associated feasts can come as a surprise. The medieval attitude to Christmas can come as an even bigger surprise, for although it formed a high point in the calendar, the Church did not endow it with anything like the significance that it has today. Having said that, the signs of its future importance were becoming apparent with the emergence of Nativity plays and Christmas carols, and it generated its own moveable feast, since it was preceded by a period of reflection known as Advent.

The rest of the year was peppered with a whole host of festivals celebrating particular events or religious themes. Indeed, it was possible to give every Sunday a special title. The most significant were Easter, Trinity and Palm Sunday, but there were also Invocabit, Gaudete, Laetare, Cantate and Quasimodo Sunday, which were named

33. A Palm Sunday procession from a French pontifical, c. 1346–1378. A bishop in vestments and mitre processing with clerics and a layman, all carrying 'palm' fronds. Egerton MS 931, f. 255.

after the first word of the opening psalm, or introit, sung at the beginning of the mass that day as the priest proceeded to the altar. It was no accident that so many of these feasts fell on a Sunday, for this was the day that the Church dedicated to the solemn and public worship of God, and yet this bears testament to the Church's attempt to elevate the status of Sunday and consecrate it to divine worship. This process ultimately established the week as an important subdivision of time, for although the seven-day week was both a Jewish and Imperial Roman custom, it was the Church that ensured that it became established throughout medieval Christian Europe. The sanctification of Sunday had social implications, for certain activities were regarded as unfitting for a Sunday, and were therefore discouraged by the Church and even banned by the secular authorities. Of course some feasts had fixed

34. Scene from an English pontifical, c. 1420–1430, showing a Bishop moving a saint's relics to a niche in an altar. Lansdowne MS 451, f. 136v.

dates and could therefore fall on any day of the week, not just Sunday. One of the most important was the Annunciation of the Blessed Virgin Mary, or Lady Day. This fell on the 25th March, since the Annunciation marked Christ's conception, which occurred nine months before Christmas, and was regarded as the beginning of the calendar year in England until 1752, when January 1st became accepted as the official New Year's Day. The rest of the Church's fixed feasts were mainly saints' days, as the date on which a saint had died was often well known, and, if not, was established by the Church. Similarly, if the physical remains of a saint were ceremonially moved, or translated, to a place suitable for veneration (34), the date was fixed and commemorated.

As a result of all this, the year was liberally sprinkled with more or less important festivals and feasts. Indeed, due to the importance and complexity of the medieval Church's calendar, it became common to provide calendar tables at the beginning of certain liturgical and devotional books, such as breviaries and hours, in order to highlight feasts for both churchmen and laymen. These tables typically listed the important festivals month by month and provided information that allowed moveable feasts to be calculated. In order to differentiate between major and minor feasts the scribe often used different colours: black for the minor feasts; red, blue and gold for the major feasts. This gives rise to the expression 'red letter day' for an important celebration, since many medieval scribes indicated major feasts by writing the calendar entries in red, rather than black (35, overleaf).

Following pages: 35. Red letter feasts for December, followed by the Beatus page beginning the psalms, from a French breviary made at the beginning of the fourteenth century. A breviary contained the services necessary for the Regular clergy to celebrate their daily round of worship. Yates Thompson MS 8, ff. 6v–7.

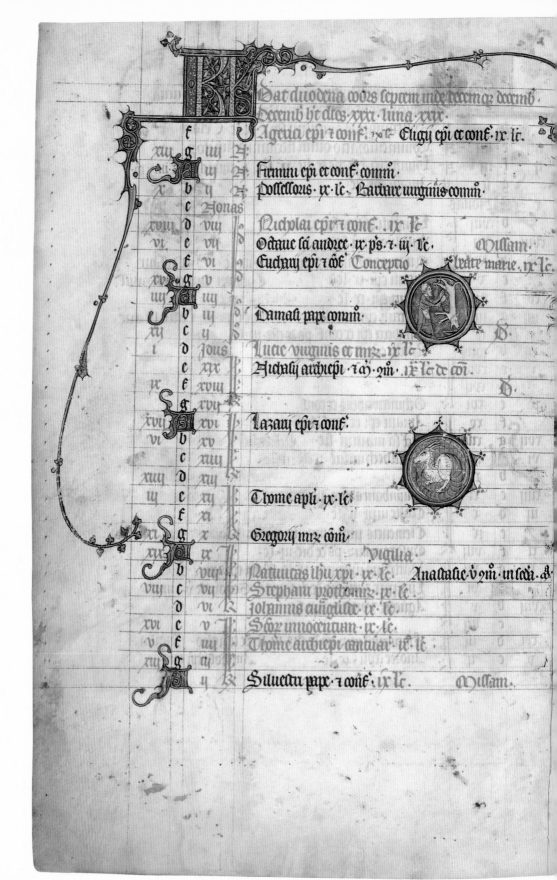

Sat duodena cedrs septem inde decem q̃ decemb
Decemb̃ hr dies xxxi luna xxix

	f		Agricia epi ꞇ conf̃ ·	Eligij epi et conf̃ · ix lc̃
xiiij	g	iiij	℣	
	A	iij	℣	Firmini epi et conf̃ · comm̃
x	b	y	℣	Possessoris · ix · lc̃ · Barbare uirginis comm̃
	c	Nonas		
xviij	d	viij		Nicholai epi ꞇ conf̃ · ix · lc̃
vi	e	vij		Octaue sc̃i andree · ix · p̃s · ꞇ · iij · lc̃ · Willam
	f	vi		Euchary epi ꞇ cõf̃ Conceptio beate marie · ix lc̃
xiiij	g	iiij		
iiij	A	iiij		Damasi pape comm̃
xij	b	iij		
l	c	Jdus		Luce uirginis et mr̃z · ix lc̃
	d	xix		Nichasij archiepi · ꞇ m̃ · m̃ · ix lc̃ de cõi
ix	e	xviij		
	f	xvij		
xvij	A	xvi		Lazari epi ꞇ conf̃
vi	b	xv		
	c	xiiij		
xiiij	d	xiij		
iij	e	xij		Thome apli · ix lc̃
	f	xi		
xi	g	x		Gregory mr̃z cõm̃
xix	A	ix		Vigilia
	b	viij		Natiuitas ihu xp̃i · ix · lc̃ Anastasie ℣ m̃ · in scd̃a ℞
vij	c	vij		Stephani prothom̃r̃z · ix · lc̃
	d	vi		Johannis eungliste · ix · lc̃
xvi	e	v		Scõr innocentium · ix · lc̃
v	f	iiij		Thome archiepi cantuar · ix · lc̃
	g	iij		
xiij	A	ij		Siluestri pape · ꞇ conf̃ · ix lc̃ · Willam

Adoremus dominum qui fecit nos. Venite.

Beatus vir qui non abijt in consilio impioꝛ: et in via peccatoꝛ non stetit. et in cathedra pestilentie non sedit. Sed in lege domini voluntas eius: et in lege eius meditabitur die ac nocte. Erit tanquam lignum quod plantatum est secus decursus aquarum: quod fructum suum dabit in tempore suo. Et folium eius non defluet: et omnia quecumque faciet semper prosperabuntur. Non sic impij non sic: sed tanquam pulvis: quem proicit ventus a facie terre. Ideo non resurgunt impij in iudicio: neque peccatores in consilio iustoꝛ. Quoniam novit dominus viam iustoꝛ: et iter impioꝛ peribit.

Quare fremuerunt gentes: et populi meditati sunt inania. Astiterunt reges terre et principes convenerunt in unum: adversus dominum: et adversus christum eius. Dirumpamus vincula eoꝛ: et proiciamus a nobis iugum ipsoꝛ. Qui habitat in celis irridebit eos: et dominus subsannabit eos. Tunc loquetur ad eos in ira sua: et in furore suo conturbabit eos. Ego autem constitutus sum rex ab eo super syon montem sanctum eius: predicans preceptum eius. Dominus dixit ad me filius meus es tu: ego hodie genui te. Postula a me et dabo tibi gentes hereditatem tuam: et possessionem tuam terminos terre. Reges eos in virga ferrea: tanquam vas figuli confringes eos. Et nunc reges intelligite: erudimini qui iudicatis terram.

CHURCH AND LAITY
DEVOTION, PILGRIMAGE AND POPULAR FEASTS

Thus far, we have examined the structure of the medieval Church and its influence upon medieval society. But it is also necessary to view the Church from the perspective of the laity if one hopes to get a more complete picture. To fully understand the religious world of the Middle Ages it is necessary to understand that many people were genuinely motivated by feelings of religious piety. Illuminated manuscripts stand testament to these deep feelings, because many, such as the Book of Hours, were produced for the purposes of private devotion. Many contain images that emphasise the spiritual, for they frequently show their owners engaged in private prayer (36). On a more prosaic level, these manuscripts show how much individuals were prepared to invest in items used for private devotion, for their creation would have required a huge amount of time, effort, skill and, above all, money. Detailed accounts relating to the production of a service book known as the Westminster, or Litlyngton, Missal, which was made between 1383 and 1387 for Westminster Abbey, where it remains to this day, show that it cost a little under £40. This was a considerable sum at a time when a chantry priest – a cleric employed to pray for the soul of someone who had died – might receive about £4 a year! However, individuals would only rarely be able to spend such sums. In fact chantry priests also testify to the importance of religion for the individual, since many people left considerable sums in their wills in order to employ them. Even the churches and cathedrals owe much to individual acts of religiously motivated generosity, for most were constructed and decorated as a result of private donations.

The medieval concept of sainthood is also best understood when viewed from the perspective of the laity. By the end of the Middle Ages the papacy had established its right to confirm the saintly status of individuals through a centralised process called canonisation, involving an assessment of the candidate's life and of the miracles ascribed to them after death. But it could not entirely remove the element of popular acclaim that characterised the establishment of saints during the Early Middle Ages. As a result, medieval saints were popular figures, even if their popularity was

36. Book of Hours from France, mid-fifteenth century, showing the owner praying to the Virgin Mary. *Additional MS 27697, f. 19.*

localised, such as Saint Frideswide of Oxford. The basis of medieval sainthood rested on the belief that certain individuals lived lives that were touched by God, and could therefore act as a bridge between the people and God, even after their deaths. Such individuals could be appealed to as divine intermediaries through the process of prayer, and even their physical remains and possessions were venerated, just as the physical items associated with Christ were treated with reverence. The most visible manifestation of these beliefs was the act of pilgrimage, which saw the faithful undertake journeys to places of religious significance (37). The most famous place of pilgrimage was Jerusalem, and the surrounding area is still referred to as the Holy Land, due to its association with Christ and the Bible. But there were other centres of pilgrimage, including Rome, Santiago de Compostella, the Spanish town containing the shrine of Saint James, known in Latin as Sanctus Iacobus, and Canterbury, in England, where Thomas Becket was murdered in 1170 (38).

37. Pilgrims depicted leaving Canterbury, in an addition by a Flemish artist (c. 1525) to an unfinished English copy of John Lydgate's poems, c. 1465. Royal MS 18 D ii, f. 148.

38. The martyrdom of Thomas Becket from a collection of material relating to Becket made at Christ Church, Canterbury, c. 1190. The praying figures, bottom right, are Becket's murderers, but his tomb quickly attracted pilgrims. Cotton MS Claudius B ii, f. 341.

Some feasts even betray something of the conflict that existed between popular and authorised forms of devotion. The feast of All Saints' Day, or All Hallows' Day, was celebrated by the Church on the 1st November to commemorate the community of saints not specifically mentioned in the calendar and was included in many devotional works, such as the Chevalier Hours depicted overleaf (39). But it was bound up with the unsanctioned festival of Hallowe'en, or All Hallows' Evening. The roots of Hallowe'en are probably to be found in a pre-Christian festival marking the beginning of Winter. The Church probably set the date of All Saints' Day so as to reinterpret and Christianise the pagan festival, and present it as the dark before the dawn of the feast of All Saints. However, despite its best efforts, the popular pagan element still survives. Another popular celebration, whose origins are Christian rather than pagan, is the one now known in England as Pancake Tuesday.

39. *The community of saints, marking the opening of the text for the commemoration of*
All Saints in the Chevalier Hours, c. 1420. Additional MS 16997, f. 137.

Because Easter was preceded by the forty-day period of fasting and contemplation,
known as Lent, people exploited the chance to indulge themselves before it began.
The last opportunity for indulgence always fell on a Tuesday, since Lent began on a
Wednesday, and because Lent was a period of fast people tended to concentrate upon
eating. The consumption of perishable and fatty foods, such as eggs and milk, led to
the custom of the pancake and prompted the term Mardi Gras (literally meaning
Tuesday of fat), whilst the prohibition of eating meat during Lent led to the term
carnival (from Latin, *carnis*, flesh or meat, and *vale*, farewell). The alternative name of
Shrove Tuesday comes from an Old English term relating to the confession of sin,
traditionally undertaken before Lent.

The relationship between ecclesiastical and secular celebration was quite complex. The ceremony of coronation had a strongly religious dimension, and was conducted by senior churchmen, as can be seen in an illustrated coronation service book, made in 1365 for King Charles V of France (40). Moreover, essentially religious celebrations were becoming secularised, partly because the laity was beginning to play a more important role. Although the Church had an antagonistic attitude towards theatre during the Early Middle Ages, it began to introduce dramatic interludes into some of its religious services. By the fifteenth century these dramas had escaped the confines of Church ceremonial and had passed into the hands of the laity as public performances known as Mysteries and Miracle plays. Typical of these religious dramas is a cycle of plays associated with York, which was organised by the town's guilds. Lay participation in religious ceremony increased in other areas too. Although the Church developed new and increasingly elaborate musical forms and made them an important element of religious celebration, the performance of music was originally restricted to the clergy. But lay participation began to increase towards the end of the period,

40. The blessing of the French royal banners, symbolising the Church's legitimization and sanctification of Secular authority, from the coronation book of Charles V of France, 1365. Cotton MS Tiberius B viii, f. 73.

until groups of musicians became a common feature of popular Church celebration (41). Indeed, religious festivals were becoming increasingly secular affairs, and were beginning to be transformed from holy days into holidays.

41. *A Flemish breviary, made before 1497, showing King David, with musicians. Although this is a biblical scene, the musicians are portrayed as fifteenth-century laymen on the steps of a cathedral. Additional MS 18851, f. 184v.*

CHURCH AND LAITY
THE LAITY'S CONTACT WITH THE CHURCH

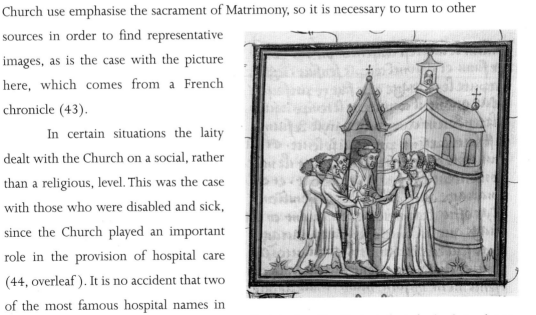

The image presented so far has suggested that the relationship between the laity and the Church was a close one. But this was often not the case. For one thing, although the faithful were expected to attend mass on a regular basis, it was not the weekly obligation familiar to many today. Moreover, in contrast to modern practice, the faithful were merely observers, not participants, for mass was performed in Latin and was celebrated by a priest with his back to the congregation (42, overleaf). An interesting legacy of this may be the expression 'hocus pocus', meaning something magical, for it has been argued that it comes from a corruption of the words 'Hoc est corpus', or 'Here is the body', which formed part of the sacrament of the Eucharist. If so, it shows that the focus of the Latin mass was misunderstood and regarded as a mysterious act. What is more, the laity's dealings with the Church were often less elaborate than the pictorial sources suggest. Marriages, for instance, were typically blessed at the church door, without the need for elaborate ceremonial or vestments. However, manuscripts produced for Church use emphasise the sacrament of Matrimony, so it is necessary to turn to other sources in order to find representative images, as is the case with the picture here, which comes from a French chronicle (43).

In certain situations the laity dealt with the Church on a social, rather than a religious, level. This was the case with those who were disabled and sick, since the Church played an important role in the provision of hospital care (44, overleaf). It is no accident that two of the most famous hospital names in England owe their origins to medieval Church foundations, namely St Barts and

43. *A simple wedding blessing in front of a church. French copy of Jean de Vignay's chronicle entitled* Miroir Historial, *late fourteenth century. Lansdowne MS 1179, f. 24.*

42. Priest celebrating mass, with his back to the congregation, from a Book of Hours, Flanders, c. 1492. Additional MS 25698, f. 2.

Bedlam. Saint Bartholomew's Hospital was an Augustinian foundation established in 1123, whilst Bedlam, established in 1247, was a priory hospital under the order of St Mary of Bethlehem. The latter seems to have specialised in the care of the insane as early as the fifteenth century and gave rise to the term bedlam, due to a local corruption of its abbreviated name of Bethlem. Those seeking an education also had need to deal with the Church, since most schools were ecclesiastical foundations, and were either run by cathedrals or individual churchmen, typically a chantry priest.

44. *Injured peasants seeking the support of the Church — indicating the Church's social, rather than religious, role. Decretals of Pope Gregory IX, illuminated in England, c. 1330–1340. Royal MS 10 E iv, f. 197.*

In fact, one of the laity's most significant areas of contact with the Church may have been financial, rather than religious. The tithe (from the Old English *teotha*, or tenth) was a traditional Church claim to one tenth of the crops, produce and profits of the laity, which was made so that the clergy could be supported by the community of the faithful, and could therefore devote themselves entirely to their religious tasks. However, by the thirteenth century the tithe was not a voluntary contribution but an established ecclesiastical tax, whose payment was enforced by secular legislation throughout Europe (45). In addition, the clergy claimed other rights, such as a portion of the first day of harvest (46, overleaf). But it was the Church's general tendency to charge for its services that coloured the laity's dealings with it. The abbey church of Sherborne was burned in 1437 during a riot caused by the monastery's financial monopoly over baptisms, which angered the local parish priest and parishioners.

45. *A priest receiving tithes – ecclesiastical taxes imposed by secular legislation – from parishioners. Tithes were levied throughout Europe, as shown in this scene from a Spanish copy of the Law Code of Alfonso X of Castile and Leon, 1275–1300. Additional MS 20787, f. 106v.*

But even if the Church was increasingly seen as a socially powerful institution, rather than a purely religious force, its influence upon the laity was still enormous. The Church's power can be detected in a number of modern English words and expressions. For instance, the Middle English word for a prayer was *bede*, from which we derive the expression 'I bid you goodbye', or as a medieval English speaker would have understood it, 'I pray that God be with you'. By extension the word *bede* became associated with the string of rounded ornaments strung together as an aid to counting prayers, now known as a rosary, which eventually gave rise to the modern word bead, meaning a small globular object such as is found in a necklace. The rosary probably played a part in the origins of another common English word, gaudy, meaning something ornate and showy, since it became common medieval practice to indicate the important prayers or *bedes* on a rosary, referred to in Middle English as *gaudys* (probably from the Latin word *gaudeo*, to rejoice), by using more highly decorated, and thus gaudy, beads. The survival of words of frustration, such as 'hell' and 'damnation', betray medieval society's preoccupation with the afterlife, and

46. The laity bringing the 'first fruits' into the church, a legal requirement
set out in the law book of Alphonso X of Aragon. The claim to 'first fruits'
also applied in England. Additional MS 20787, f. 104v.

with the fate that awaited those who did not heed the word of the Church. But the
strength of this obsession is, once again, fully revealed in the illuminated manuscripts
of the period, for many contain powerful images of sinners being condemned to the
eternal fires of hell. These acted as a powerful visual reminder of the need to live a
Christian life, and often showed that neither king nor cleric could assume that they
would be spared (47, overleaf).

The images to be found in manuscripts provide an extremely valuable insight into the
world of the medieval Church. The vast majority of these images are to be found in
works of a purely religious nature, such as service books used by members of the
clergy and the devotional works of the laity. But the pervasive power of the Church
during the Middle Ages was such that many other works, including chronicles, legal
texts, romances and travellers' tales, include pictures that help to throw light upon the

Following pages: 47. The damned, many of whom are churchmen, consigned to hell, reflecting the medieval
preoccupation with the afterlife and suggesting that an anti-clerical feeling exsisted during this period.
French Book of Hours, c. 1407. Additional MS 29433, f. 89.

48. Vincent of Beauvais, a Dominican monk writing in his study, is often misused as a representation of a Carmelite because of his black and white habit. Flemish copy of Jean de Vignay's Miroir Historial, 1470–1483. Royal MS 14 E i, f. 3.

medieval Church. To those interested in gaining an insight into the distant world of the Middle Ages, all of these visual sources are of interest. But it is worth noting that the manuscripts sometimes provide a misleading image, and occasionally need to be assessed with care. A particular image of a monk wearing black and white habit has often been used as a general image of a Carmelite monk, but the figure in question is Vincent de Beauvais, a Dominican, and the image is an author portrait at the

49. *John the Baptist, baptising a follower and attended by Minor clerics in garments typical of the twelfth century, from a French roll showing scenes relating to John the Baptist. Additional MS 42497, pics. 3 and 4.*

beginning of a copy of Vincent's *Speculum Historiale* (48). Similarly, an image from a roll containing images relating to the life of St John the Baptist shows figures in white ecclesiastical garments holding candles, beside an adult being baptised in a large tub (49). Although the scene represents John the Baptist baptising his followers, the robed attendants may represent the appearance of Minor clerics as they would have looked when the picture was painted in the twelfth century. However, adult baptism was unusual at this time, since most people were baptised shortly after birth, so the accuracy of the scene is open to question. Nevertheless, despite these shortcomings, the wealth of images provided in medieval manuscripts is not only very revealing, but also truly amazing, and they give us a much better understanding of Church practice, ceremony, ornament and teaching during this time.

IMPORTANT CHURCH FEAST DAYS

Feast Day	Occasion or Theme	Date/Period Celebrated	Moveable/Fixed
Advent	Beginning of the Church year	Fourth Sunday before Christmas	Moveable
Gaudete Sunday		Third Sunday of Advent	Moveable
Christmas	Christ's Birth	25th December	Fixed
Dies Cinerum or Ash Wednesday	Commencement of Lent	40 days before Easter Sunday	Moveable
Invocabit Sunday		First Sunday of Lent	Moveable
Laetare Sunday		Fourth Sunday of Lent	Moveable
Dies Palmarum or Palm Sunday	Christ's Entry into Jerusalem	Last Sunday of Lent	Moveable
Maundy Thursday	The Last Supper	Thursday before Easter Sunday	Moveable
Good Friday	Christ's Crucifixion	Friday before Easter Sunday	Moveable
Easter Sunday	Christ's Resurrection	First Sunday after the first full moon after the Spring equinox	Moveable
Lady Day	Annunciation of the Virgin Mary	25th March	Fixed
Quasimodo Sunday		First Sunday after Easter	Moveable
Cantate Sunday		Fourth Sunday after Easter	Moveable
Ascension Thursday	Ascension of Christ to heaven	40 days after Easter Saturday	Moveable
Pentecost or Whitsunday	Apostles receive the Holy Spirit	50 days after Good Friday	Moveable
Trinity Sunday	The Holy Trinity	First Sunday after Pentecost	Moveable
Corpus Christi	The Holy Eucharist	Thursday after Trinity Sunday	Moveable
All Saints' Day	The Community of Saints	1st November	Fixed

FURTHER READING

For articles relating to specific Church terms, and to particular aspects of practice and doctrine, see *The Catholic Encyclopedia*, 17 vols. (New York, 1907–1918), subsequently revised and reprinted, and also available via the internet. F. Donald Logan, *A History of the Church in the Middle Ages* (London and New York, 2002), provides an historical overview of the Church's structure and development, with good suggestions for further reading, as does Bernard Hamilton, *Religion in the Medieval West* (London, 1986), which focuses upon religious belief. A chronological assessment of the medieval papacy's relationship with the medieval English Church can be found in C.H. Lawrence (ed.), *The English Church and the Papacy in the Middle Ages* (revised edition, Stroud, 1999), whilst R.N. Swanson, *Church and Society in Late Medieval England* (London, 1993), provides a socio-economic slant. Information about the Regular Church can be found in C.H. Lawrence, *Medieval Monasticism* (3rd edition, Harlow, 2001), and Kenneth Rowlands, *The Friars: A History of the British Medieval Friars* (Lewes, 1999). For female monasticism, see S. Thompson, *Women Religious: The Founding of English Nunneries after the Norman Conquest* (Oxford, 1991) and E. Power, *Medieval English Nunneries c.1275–1535* (Cambridge, 1922).

A good introduction to music and the Church can be found in Nicolas Bell, *Music in Medieval Manuscripts* (London, 2001), and Dunbar H. Ogden, *The Staging of Drama in the Medieval Church* (Cranbury, London and Ontario, 2002), provides a fascinating study of Church drama during the Middle Ages. For information about many of the manuscripts mentioned in this book, see J.J.G. Alexander (gen. ed.), *A Survey of Manuscripts Illuminated in the British Isles*, 6 vols. (London, 1978–1996) and F. Avril and J.J.G. Alexander (gen. eds.), *A Survey of Manuscripts Illuminated in France,* (London, 1996–).

LIST OF MANUSCRIPTS ILLUSTRATED

Images relating to the medieval Church are probably the most common subjects to be found in illuminated manuscripts. The illustrations for this book were taken from the following:

Additional MS 14805. Pontifical. Germany, late fifteenth century.

Additional MS 16997. Chevalier Hours. France (Paris), c. 1420.

Additional MS 18850. Bedford Hours. France (Paris), c. 1423.

Additional MS 18851. Isabella Breviary. Flanders (Bruges), before 1497.

Additional MS 20787. Law Code of Alfonso X of Castile and Leon. Spain (Castile or Leon), 1275–1300.

Additional MS 23923. Decretals. Italy, 1370–1381.

Additional MS 24189. *Travels of Sir John Mandeville.* Bohemia, c. 1410.

Additional MS 24642. Decretals. Italy, mid-fourteenth century.

Additional MS 25698. Book of Hours. Flanders, c. 1492.

Additional MS 27697. Saluces Hours. France (Savoy), mid-fifteenth century.

Additional MS 28784 B. Scrap Book. Flanders (Liège), late thirteenth century, and France, 1430–1450.

Additional MS 28962. Prayer Book of Alfonso V of Aragon. Aragon or Naples, c. 1442.

Additional MS 29433. Book of Hours. France (Paris), c. 1407.

Additional MS 31032. *Rationale Divinorum Officiorum,* by William Durandus. Italy, early fourteenth century.

Additional MS 39677. Pontifical, use of Mende. France, early fourteenth century.

Additional MS 42130. Luttrell Psalter. England (Lincoln diocese), c. 1325–1335.

Additional MS 42497. Scenes of the Life of John the Baptist. France (Alsace, Hohenbourg), late twelfth century.

Additional MS 49598. Benedictional of St Æthelwold. England (Winchester, Old Minster), c. 971–984.

Additional MS 49622. Gorleston Psalter. England (Gorleston?), 1310–1320.

Additional MS 57534. Processional. England (Norwich), c. 1400.

Cotton MS Claudius B ii. Life and Letters of St Thomas Becket. England (Canterbury, Christ Church), c. 1180.

Cotton MS Domitian A xvii. Psalter of Henry VI. France (Paris), c. 1400–1410, with later additions, France c. 1420.

Cotton MS Nero D i. *Lives of the Offas,* by Matthew Paris. England (St Albans), c. 1250–1259.

Cotton MS Nero D vii. Golden Book of St Albans. England (St Albans), 1380, with later additions, England (St Albans), fifteenth century.

Cotton MS Tiberius B viii, ff. 35–80. Coronation Order of Charles V of France. France (Paris), 1365.

Egerton MS 931. Pontifical. France, c. 1346–1378.

Egerton MS 1067. Pontifical. France, late fifteenth century.

Egerton MS 2019. Book of Hours. France, mid to late fifteenth century.

Egerton MS 2125. Prayerbook of the Abbess of Messines. Flanders (Bruges), 1516 or later.

Egerton MS 2849. Mortuary Roll of Lucy, Prioress of Hedingham. England (Essex, Hedingham), c. 1226.

Harley MS 2803. Worms Bible. Germany (Rhineland, Frankenthal), 1148.

Harley MS 2915. Book of Hours. England, c. 1450.

Harley MS 7026. Lovel Lectionary. England (Salisbury diocese), c. 1408.

Harley Roll Y 6. Guthlac Roll. England (Crowland?), c. 1210.

Lansdowne MS 451. Pontifical. England (London?), 1420–1430.

Lansdowne MS 1179. *Miroir Historial,* by Jean de Vignay. France, late fourteenth century.

Royal MS 1 D i. Bible of William of Devon. England (Oxford?), c. 1260–1270.

Royal MS 2 A xxii. Westminster Psalter. England (Westminster?), c. 1200, with later additions, England (Winchester), c. 1250.

Royal MS 6 E vi. *Omne Bonum.* England (London), c. 1350–1375.

Royal MS 8 G iii. *Compendium Super Bibliam,* by Peter of Aix. England (Lincoln with London additions?), before 1422.

Royal MS 10 E iv. Smithfield Decretals. Italy (?), c. 1330–1340, with added illuminations, England (London?), c. 1330–1340.

Royal MS 14 E i. *Miroir Historial,* by Jean de Vignay. Flanders (Bruges?), 1470–1483.

Royal MS 14 E iv. *Chronique d'Angleterre,* by Jean de Wavrin. Flanders (Bruges?), 1470–1480.

Royal MS 18 D ii. Collected Works of John Lydgate. England, c. 1465, with later additions, Flanders, c. 1525.

Stowe MS 17. Book of Hours. Flanders (Maastricht?), c. 1300.

Stowe MS 944. New Minster *Liber Vitae.* England (Winchester, New Minster), c. 1031.

Yates Thompson MS 8. Breviary of Marguerite de Bar (Winter portion). France (Lorraine), 1302–1304.

Yates Thompson MS 11. *La Sainte Abbaye.* France, c. 1300.

Yates Thompson MS 24. Pontifical, use of Mende. France, c. 1380.

INDEX

To my wife, Jess, and my daughter, Tara

THE AUTHOR

Justin Clegg is a Curator of Medieval Manuscripts at the British Library. A trained historian and medievalist, he now deals with illuminated and liturgical items within the Department of Manuscripts.

Front Cover Illustration:	*Clerics being ordained as porters by a bishop, who gives them keys, symbolic of their office. Italian copy of William Durandus' Rationale Divinorum Officiorum, early fourteenth century. Additional MS 31032, f. 29.*
Half-title Page:	*A marginal scene from a Maastricht Book of Hours, c. 1300, showing clerical misbehaviour, with a nun dancing to a tune played by a friar. Stowe MS 17, f. 38.*
Frontispiece:	*Dominican nuns at prayer. Illumination, c. 1420, added to a French psalter, c. 1400–1410. Cotton MS Domitian A xvii, f. 177v.*
Title Page:	*Guthlac being ordained a priest by Bishop Hedda, from a roll depicting scenes from the life of St Guthlac, England, c. 1210. Harley Roll Y 6, roundel 11.*
Page 4:	*Vigil for the dead, with marginal scenes including confession, unction, communion and burial. Parisian Book of Hours, c. 1423. Additional MS 18850, f 120.*
Back Cover:	*A priest receiving tithes from parishioners. Spanish copy of the Law Code of Alfonso X of Castile and Leon, 1275–1300. Additional MS 20787, f. 106v.*

First published 2003 by
The British Library
96 Euston Road
London NW1 2DB

British Library Cataloguing-in-Publication Data
A catalogue record for this book is available from The British Library
ISBN 0 7123 4784 4

Designed and typeset by Crayon Design, Stoke Row, Henley-on-Thames
Colour origination by Crayon Design and South Sea International Press
Printed in Hong Kong by South Sea International Press